Lost

Story written by Gill Munton
Illustrated by Tim Archbold

Speed Sounds

Consonants   *Ask children to say the sounds.*

f	l	m	n	r	s	v	z	sh	th	ng
ff	ll	mm	nn	rr	ss	ve	zz			nk
ph	le	mb	kn	wr	se		se			
					ce		s			

b	c	d	g	h	j	p	qu	t	w	x	y	ch
bb	k	dd	gg		g	pp		tt	wh			tch
	ck				ge							

Each box contains one sound but sometimes more than one grapheme.
*Focus graphemes for this story are **circled**.*

Vowels

Ask children to say the sounds in and out of order.

a	e	i	o	u	ay	ee	igh	ow
	ea					y	i	o
at	hen	in	on	up	day	see	high	blow

oo	oo	ar	or	air	ir	ou	oy
			oor				oi
			ore				
zoo	look	car	for	fair	whirl	shout	boy

Story Green Words

Ask children to read the words first in Fred Talk and then say the word.

Kay West   Ray Brooks   Jay   plump   check   sheds   stray

hay   shock   fond   glad   kiss   string   Sandy Bay   grey*

Ask children to say the syllables and then read the whole word.

vis|it   Cat|kin

Ask children to read the root first and then the whole word with the suffix.

play → playful   pray → praying

* Challenge Words

6

Vocabulary Check

Discuss the meaning (as used in the story) after the children have read each word.

	definition:	sentence:
plump	fat	*Very plump, playful black cat.*
sheds	small buildings for storing things in gardens	*Will you check your sheds?*
stray	lost	*I've got a stray cat in my shed.*
hay	dried long grass	*She's sitting in a box of hay.*
fond	to like something	*I am very fond of them.*

Red Words

Ask children to practise reading the words across the rows, down the columns and in and out of order clearly and quickly.

they	call	all	are
your	you	her	what
do	to	brother	of
were	are	they	was
who	school	want	some

Lost

Lost last Sunday:

Very plump, playful black cat called Catkin.

Will you check your sheds?

If you find her, contact Kay West

at 24 Clayton Villas.

Thank you so much for looking.

Kay West

3rd May

To Kay West

I've got a stray cat in my shed.
I think it may be Catkin!
She's sitting in a box of hay,
and she looks as if she
wants to stay in it!

I will be in at six o'clock today if you want to visit.

From Ray Brooks (33 Hilltop Way)

4th May

To Ray Brooks

Hooray! Today is such a happy day! Thank you so much for finding my Catkin! It's what I was praying for!

But it was a bit of a shock to find the kittens in the box of hay with her – a black kitten and a grey kitten!
Still, I think she will be a very good mum.
By the way, I am glad to say they are all well.

From Kay West

PS I am going on holiday on Sunday to Sandy Bay!

5th May

To Kay

I am glad Catkin and the kittens are well.
I am very fond of them.

When you go away on holiday,
will you let them all stay with me
at Hilltop Way?

From Ray

To Ray　　　　　　10th May

I am having a very good
holiday at Sandy Bay.
Are Catkin and the kittens
being good?
Do give them all a big kiss
from me!

From Kay

Mr Ray Brooks

33 Hilltop Way

Grays

Essex

13

20th May

To Kay

It's good to have you back!
I want to ask you if the grey kitten may stay with me
at Hilltop Way. When you were away, he lay on my bed
all day and played with a bit of string.
I think he wants to stay.

What do you say?
From Ray
PS I have called him Jay!

21st May

To Ray

Yes, the kitten may stay with you!
I'm glad you have called him Jay.
When you go on holiday
he must stay in Clayton Villas
with me, Catkin
and his brother, Ray.
(Yes, I have called my kitten Ray!)

From Kay

Questions to talk about

Ask children to TTYP each question using 'Fastest finger' (FF) or 'Have a think' (HaT).

p.9 (FF) How does Kay describe Catkin?

p.10 (FF) What does Ray find in his shed?

p.11 (HaT) How do you think Kay felt when she realised Catkin had had kittens?

      (FF) How many kittens does Catkin have?

p.12 (FF) Where does Ray want the kittens to stay while Kay is on holiday?

p.13 (FF) What does Kay want Ray to give the kittens?

p.14 (FF) What does Ray call the grey kitten?

p.15 (FF) Who does Kay name her kitten after?

Questions to read and answer

(Children complete without your help.)

1. Where was Catkin sitting?
   Catkin was sitting in **a box of hay / a red bag / a big cup**.

2. Where did Kay go?
   Kay went to **stay with her mum / on holiday / to the shops**.

3. Where did Catkin and the kittens stay when Kay was away?
   They stayed with **Gran / Dad / Ray**.

4. What did the grey kitten play with?
   The grey kitten played with **a frog / a teddy / a bit of string**.

5. What are the kittens called?
   The kittens are called **Tom and Fred / Jay and Ray / Pat and Sid**.

Speedy Green Words

Ask children to practise reading the words across the rows, down the columns and in and out of order clearly and quickly.

check	find	happy	kitten
holiday	being	very	playful
thank	much	looking	stay
box	black	way	back
say	with	must	from